A Permanent Solution

Rescue Our Liberties;
Regain Our Pride

By:

Joe Carrion

authorHOUSE®

AuthorHouse™
1663 Liberty Drive
Bloomington, IN 47403
www.authorhouse.com
Phone: 1-800-839-8640

Published by AuthorHouse 2/15/2012

ISBN: 978-1-4520-7568-6 (e)
ISBN: 978-1-4520-7569-3 (sc)

Library of Congress Control Number: 2010913717

This book is printed on acid-free paper.

NOTE FROM THE AUTHOR

Most of this book was written more than twenty years ago, shortly after my retirement from business. Unfortunately, everything written at that time was apparently lost due to a computer accident. I am not a good typist, and certainly not very good with computers. So, in frustration, I abandoned the project at that time. Then, recently, while going through some old papers, I found a hard copy of the first draft which I thought had been lost. Reading that old document revived many of my old fears and apprehensions, and awakened a sense of urgency to finish what I had started so long ago.

Much has happened over the last twenty years, but nothing to improve the situation that worried me before. On the contrary, recent events have confirmed my misgivings, and it seemed important to do something, and not just sit idly by.

I am now in my mid-eighties and initially had trouble finding the energy to start anew. But, my son and daughters not only encouraged me to do so, they also helped me actively in the many details that must be taken care of in order to bring a project like this to completion. I really appreciate their contribution.

I have tried to make as few modifications to the original manuscript as possible, although obviously some things have had to be updated. As I have done so, I am more convinced than ever than something has to be done NOW.

Joe Carrión

INTRODUCTION

It's been more than thirty-five years since I suffered what was undoubtedly the most traumatic experience of my life. A life-threatening incident which made me re-appraise my priorities in life, but which also created a new awareness in me about the virtues and the greatness of this great country of ours. It renewed in me the feelings of duty and urgency to do my part in preserving our liberties and our democratic ways.

But this new awareness also created a growing anxiety as, over the years, I seemed to discern a subtle but inexorable erosion of our individual liberties; a gradual but continuous shift of power from *"We the people"* to an ever growing government bureaucracy which, in my opinion, is beginning to resemble a quasi-socialistic system. I believe we need to make a course correction before this new direction takes us to where we do not want to go.

More than twenty years have passed since my retirement, and I now have the helpless feeling that I am sitting idly by while things continue to deteriorate. I would still like to do something worthwhile, so I decided to put some of my thoughts on paper in the hope that they might do some good. And yet, I debated with myself strongly before starting on this, my first attempt at writing. I feel I have something to say, but I have read enough to know that good subject matter poorly expressed will be put aside, and it was a temptation to find somebody with better writing talents to put my thoughts in print. I was afraid however that somehow the specific ideas that I wanted to convey might be distorted or disguised, and that would defeat the whole purpose.

I have always had a tendency towards oversimplification. Embellishment was never my forte. In school, in business, in sports, and even in everyday conversation my passion for directness and disregard for inconsequential details has often gotten me into trouble. I abhor small talk and my custom of disregarding unimportant (to me) matters so often makes me forget names, faces, or events that it has been a continuous source of embarrassment. But that is the way I am and the choice was mine to make.

So in characteristic fashion I decided it would be **my way** or not at all and, at the risk of having it ignored after the first paragraph, I set out to use my straight-to-the-point and unembellished style to express my concerns and offer my suggestions. This, then, is the result. I am sure nobody will label it a literary masterpiece, but hopefully it will convey a message of some importance to people who , like me, love this great country that we live in.

PROLOGUE

It was about 8:30 in the morning on a bright clear day in San Juan, Puerto Rico on a Friday in April of 1972, when I was kidnapped. I was just leaving the house when a man approached my car waving a large manila envelope with my name obviously written across the front of it. It was so unexpected that I made it absurdly easy for him. I rolled down the window of the car to take the offered envelope, and instead I watched him come in gun in hand. Thus began what was to be a terrifying experience that seriously threatened my life and which permanently changed my thinking about a lot of things.

I was taken blindfolded to a place that appeared to be a basement or a garage office. He first had me phone my secretary at the bank to cancel all my appointments telling her that I would be taking care of some business outside of the office. He then had me call another department in the bank to instruct them to prepare a large sum of money to be transferred, stating that I would stop by to pick it up personally. It did no good to explain to him that the bank did not do business in this manner. He just told me to make it sound plausible because my life depended on having the bank follow instructions to the letter. By this time we had spent some time together and it was apparent to me that once he had his hands on that money, my chances of being left alive to be able to identify him were pretty slim.

I made up a story that I felt would sound logical to his criminal mind but which would be sure to alert the bank officials. At the time, our bank was involved in a large much-publicized lawsuit so I told the bank officials the money was to be used as a secret payoff to the opposing attorney to get the suit settled. As agreed, we made the pick up of the money, and predictably also acquired an escort of F.B.I. and other law enforcement agents.

The next few hours were truly frightening for me as my role changed from one of kidnap victim to that of a hostage. I spent most of the day with a gun to my head while the officers kept their distance. I cannot say enough good things about the F.B.I. My safety was apparently uppermost on their list of objectives and keep me alive they did.

The kidnapper's plans had to change drastically. He had hoped to remain anonymous and enjoy the money, but now he had been identified and had to get away. He negotiated for an airplane to be ready for us at midnight. There were some very anxious moments at the small airport in the city of Ponce, but finally sometime about 12:30 a.m. we were airborne heading for an up to a then undisclosed but predictable destination: communist Cuba. The trip was uneventful and we landed at dawn.

The kidnapper was taken by the Cuban authorities, the money confiscated, the two pilots were led in a different direction; and without warning I discovered that I was to be given the treatment of a "guest" of the Cuban government. I was taken to a large comfortable house in what used to be one of the exclusive residential sections in Havana and enjoyed five days of almost complete solitude. On two occasions, men in uniform came to ask questions. I was free to roam about the house and the grounds and talk about inconsequential subjects with the man who did the cooking. There was a library that consisted almost entirely of communist propaganda. I even tried to read some of it but I could find nothing to hold my attention. There was a television set, a black and white Russian model that would pick up only two local government stations. I enjoyed a good local baseball game on Sunday afternoon and watched a couple of old movies, but not much else was worth even turning on the set. News broadcasts had too much propaganda and very little news. After listening many times about which brigade was doing well in the sugar cane harvest, even the news failed to draw my attention to the "idiot box". The hours passed slowly and there was a lot of time for thinking. Only when a man named

Quero came around and we had a chance to talk did the clock seem to move at its normal speed.

I never did find out if Quero was his first or last name. He was the person in charge of my well-being and although he obviously had duties elsewhere he came every day and for long periods of time we talked. Conversation was tentative and strained at first, but gradually we both loosened up and talked more freely. And in a strange way we became friendly if not friends. He was intelligent and well informed and the subjects ranged from political ideology to baseball to economics. He certainly did not convert me to his way of thinking and I'm sure that I did not convert him to mine. Yet probably some change in both of our outlooks took place as a result.

THROUGH THE LOOKING GLASS

I sometimes wonder if that period of inactivity in Cuba actually took place. It doesn't seem real to me as I try to bring into focus all of the details of my unplanned vacation. I'm sure they meant to give me the V.I.P. treatment, but I felt like a prisoner in every sense of the word. There was no communication with the outside world and no information, as to if and when I was to be permitted to return home. Of course gone was that feeling of almost blind panic, which dominated me while in the hands of the kidnapper. But now a feeling of uncertainty and apprehension prevailed, even though logic told me that they had no reason to keep me and would soon send me back home. It was being left alone that made my mind work overtime in useless speculation.

It's no wonder that I welcomed those sessions with Quero. But even though I enjoyed his company and learned something of what was going on from him, his words added to the feeling of unreality that permeated throughout my stay in Cuba. I felt as if I had entered a different world, one with a completely different set of values. As if right and wrong as I knew them had been switched on me. Everything in that environment seemed to be just the opposite of things as I knew them to be. Every television program proclaimed Cuba as the "First Free Territory in America". One of the few programs that I watched was apparently a locally produced series that glorified the terrorists as the heroes. Looking for something to read, I picked up a book on Cuban history. Although history is not my strongest subject, it soon became apparent that the history had been rewritten with some peculiar role reversals in the process.

But most disturbing of all, was the realization that the things that we only suspect and often dismiss as improbable about communist plots were not only true, but that they were not considered to be clandestine or denied in any way. They were discussed in a matter of fact way as part of their stated program.

Our first words on this subject were tentative. I commented on how well informed he was on our political situation in Puerto Rico. We were approaching our general elections and he had been evaluating the relative chances of each candidate and expressing an opinion on the differences in their platforms. He explained that it was part of his obligations to stay on top of the political climate in Puerto Rico; this was part of their national policy. "What policy is that?" I inquired. He explained: "It is our mission to export the revolution". I asked what that could possibly have to do with Puerto Rico. He proceeded to put things in perspective by explaining that it was no secret that Cuba and the U.S.A. were enemies, but recognizing that Cuba could not hope to defeat the U.S. in an open conflict, they were working diligently on a program of infiltrating and undermining the U.S. institutions in an effort to accomplish the same results. Puerto Rico is simply part of the U.S. and as such is fair game for their plan. It might even merit some special attention under the theory that it could be considered to be a weak spot or a sort of Achilles heel in our system.

I wanted to get more specific so he obliged by explaining patiently that there are three general targets for infiltration in all locations throughout the United States: The school system or more specifically the faculties of the universities, the labor movement, and the communications media. As I continued to probe, he expressed his opinion that it was going very well. The object of their plan as he explained it was to enlighten the people about the flaws in our system. To point out the inequities that result from our capitalist economy where "the rich get richer and the poor get poorer". To promote the standard Marxist line that the fruits of labor should be distributed according to need. To have our own citizens demand from government additional curbs on all special interest groups. To encourage and promote every possible cause that might result in embarrassment to the establishment, or which could alienate any group against the elected officials. And in general to promote discontent ultimately leading to civil disobedience. They would not have to defeat us. The people of the U.S., he insisted, could be maneuvered into doing it to themselves. It was just a matter of time. Again he mused that it was going very well.

I was frankly shocked more by the openness with which he explained their strategy than by the words themselves. Did he really think that it would be that easy? My rejection of all of his claims of success was instinctive. I'm a firm believer in the American way of life. There is too much inherent strength in our democratic system. I've seen it rebound time and time again after each setback. Its apparent vacillation and roundabout way of reaching momentous decisions has proved to be its strength rather than its weakness. Continuous criticism from abroad has almost always been colored with envy. Surely this little man with his soft voice and quiet manner was grossly mistaken! He'd better be. Yet some very disturbing thoughts nagged at me. Could we really be maneuvered into weakening our basic structure in some manner? My instincts answered "no". But something still tugged at me.

I finally nailed it down. The disturbing thought was that with or without encouragement from them we might unwittingly be doing it to ourselves. No wonder the thought disturbed me. I never thought they could do a good job of managing their own affairs much less manipulate ours. But all on our own, we certainly were capable of forgetting the lessons of history and making the kind of mistakes that others could take advantage of. They obviously were very happy with their progress and at least they felt there was tangible evidence to support their claims of success. Could it be that we were unwittingly playing into their hands by our apathy and our carelessness? Was there a weakness in our system that our enemies could take advantage of which could eventually or inevitably lead to our downfall? My instincts still answered "no". I had always been aware of the threat of communism, but my conviction that our system is so far superior to any other always kept any apprehension from surfacing. Yet the thought that we could be inadvertently and through our own apathy be sabotaging ourselves would not go away.

Although Quero spoke with great candor about their plans, I believe he sensed that my reaction to his words was greater than I was trying to let on. After the second day, the subjects changed subtly and we discussed at great length the master plans they were working on for economic recovery. He deplored the mistake they had made of allowing all the "technicians" to leave the country. He explained that this had delayed the recovery but he expressed confidence that ultimately they would succeed. The economic aspects normally would have been of the outmost interest to me, but now they failed to hold my attention. Their carefully planned strategy sounded cumbersome and doomed to failure or at best likely to achieve only limited success. I pointed out what my free market educated mind believed were flaws in their plans, but my heart wasn't in it. I truly had heard more than I wanted to hear and I could concentrate on nothing but going home.

I now had another compelling reason for ending this whole episode in my life. I needed to reevaluate my thinking. I had to get away from this strange setting with its upside down distorted values. The storybook quality of that environment had come too soon after my bizarre adventure and I found that I was doubting myself and many of my deep rooted ideas. I had to get back home where the sanity of family and familiar surroundings could put things in proper perspective and help me to differentiate between absurdity and concern.

At last the news came. After four days in Cuba, Quero informed me that he would pick me up early the next morning to drive me to the airport. I was up and dressed before six and waited impatiently for the start of my return. I was reunited with the crew of the airplane at the airport and to me it was like the first of other celebrations to come. They had been kept at a local hotel and we swapped stories as we waited for clearance. I felt very close to those two pilots. After all, I had had no choice in any of the things that had happened to me, but they had courageously volunteered for my sake and, as a result, had been subjected to the same uncertainties and apprehensions as I, and they had been deprived of the comforts of home and the company of their families for the same extended period of time. Truly a remarkable sacrifice on my behalf.

There were some last minute delays but finally we were permitted to leave. The flight back was not without drama. The airplane was a De Havilland Heron; a twenty passenger, four engine craft belonging to the largest commuter airline in Puerto Rico. When the time came for take-off the pilot discovered that none of the electrical systems were working. In fact there was no electricity at all in the entire plane even with the engines running. The Cuban mechanics were unfamiliar with the airplane and could not help us. The pilot made a decision to go anyway if they would let us. He explained that the landing gear was hydraulically operated and that all of the electrical systems were strictly for backup. Of course we would have no communications and only a compass for navigation so we would change our destination to Miami for the shorter flight.

I never would have thought that I could enjoy heading out for open water and watch the shoreline disappear behind us under those conditions, but the flight was truly a delight. We were already over water when the pilot mentioned that we were supposed to go to Miami International Airport and that he hoped that he could find it because he didn't have the right maps and he had never been to Miami. I laughed and told him that Miami was like home to me, to show me the shoreline and I would point the way. In Miami they knew we were coming and make it easy for us. We were home.

"TONGUE IN CHEEK"

Adjustment to normal life after my adventure came slowly. At first it was all celebrating. The incident had attracted wide media attention and I found that I had been the beneficiary of prayers and good wishes from most people in Puerto Rico. I tried to show my appreciation, but support and efforts on my behalf had been so widespread that I could not possibly get around to thanking as many people as I would have liked. I came away from this emotional experience with the deep conviction that more than any other single thing, the combined power of so many prayers had been the dominant force in my safe return. I vowed never again to give up hope (as I had several times during that first day) and certainly never to lose my faith in God.

I took a short vacation with my family and then tried to find my place in the old routine of things. Outwardly it was easy. People had been so good to me and to my family that I had a great feeling of belonging. This was truly home and it was wonderful. But gradually and inevitably I acquired a new awareness about my surroundings that was very disturbing. I had always taken for granted the fact that ours was the greatest country in the world. The idea that an objective appraisal at this time might raise a question about what had always been a certainty was unacceptable. But some signs of deterioration were there and inescapably it became apparent that even if we were still better than others, we clearly were not as good as we could be or even as good as we had been. It suddenly dawned on me just how lucky my generation had been to have seen this country at its best. I wondered if younger generations could have the same feeling of awe and pride and appreciation and even smugness at our own supremacy. I felt the urge to tell the world the way I felt. I wanted everyone to feel the way I did.

But inevitably I became guilty of the very thing I was getting ready to criticize. Adjustment meant going back to work and very quickly the problems of the moment, and the demands of my job made me put aside for a later time any ideas I might have had about flag waving or voicing my concerns, and certainly about leading any crusades of reform. What did I hope to accomplish anyway? Clearly there are a lot of things out there that are not as they should be. And hopefully there are a lot of people out there that share these same concerns. I would have loved to think that I could somehow channel the efforts of these concerned citizens and turn them into a positive plan of action, but I realized I had no plan. Certainly nothing anybody else could get enthused about. We don't need slogans. We certainly do not need to sell people on the virtues of being "better". Noble purposes and lofty goals are fine, but without specific plans they are no more than "pep" rallies. So I put such thought aside and resumed my work routine.

But the doubts remained there with me in the background, even though I was not even sure if my concerns were indeed real or if I had merely been left with a touch of paranoia after my harrowing experience. I consciously pushed these thought into the background, but they stayed with me during the years that ensued and inevitably affected my outlook and my appreciation of the world around me.

Was there in fact enough deterioration for it to be a cause for concern? And could this deterioration be diagnosed as a trend which if not reversed could eventually jeopardize our way of life? Could it be that our system was so fragile that mere carelessness on our part would cause it to weaken and tumble? Would future students of history analyze the rise and fall of the U.S. as inevitable much as we now recall the Roman Empire? Of course this type of speculation was pointless. I needed analysis not speculation, logic not panic. Paranoia or not I was convinced a problem existed.

My concern had started with the fear that our democratic way of life might be in jeopardy. And over the years that followed I became increasingly aware that our government was growing at a fast pace and my concern increased with the conviction that this represented a subtle shift towards a less democratic and more socialistic system. Because the only way that government grows larger and stronger is by shifting power unto itself away from the people. Whether by accident or by design the structure of our democracy was gradually being weakened and I became convinced that the process needed to be reversed. We had to somehow wade through all the inconsequential aspects of the problem and find that crucial ingredient that we must change. Democracy must grow stronger not weaker and the change (if we can find it) has to be a basic one and must strike at the very core of our structure to insure that the strength comes from within and is capable of resisting all assaults or probing from without.

The words of Quero in that lonely house were not forgotten, but they now seemed inconsequential. I never believed our principal problems to be the result of communist plots. Oh the communists are out there alright and they are trying to bring us to our knees. I had better reasons than most for taking the threat of communist activity seriously. But I was always convinced that they were never our biggest threat. The danger lay in our own apathy and shortsightedness. The type of thinking that pursues immediate goals without regard for the long-term consequences. The type of thinking that will unwittingly undermine the basic principles that are the strength of our system. The type that permits the gradual erosion of our personal liberties without realizing the consequences of what they are advocating.

When I was a young man the image of the "Ugly American" was widely publicized. It was a label that unfortunately was well earned by U.S. visitors abroad. And yet I never thought the day would come when I would look back on this American image with a slight touch of nostalgia. For, inexcusable as it was, it was an attitude born from pride. This was the time when travel was beginning to become more popular and gradually available to more people. And everywhere U.S. travelers went they found that what they had at home was better. It was a startling discovery and one that was difficult to hide. In the first place, they discovered the peace of mind they enjoyed while traveling under the protection of an American passport. The dollar was coveted everywhere. They found to their surprise that we were the envy of the world, and it was easy for them to swell up with pride and proceed to exaggerate our advantages. The perception of the average tourist, whether accurate or not, appeared to be that our modes of transportation were better than anywhere else. Our cars were bigger and more comfortable. Of course the quality of European products was always excellent, but somehow they would point out that we had a more practical approach that made acceptable quality available to everybody. Japan's efforts to mass-produce resulted in poor quality and the label "Made in Japan" became synonymous with shoddy workmanship. Punctuality with us was a way of life and it was a shock to see it was not everywhere so. Latin America was the land of "mañana" and although the people there were always polite, the results were sadly lacking. Our hotels catered to our kind of service and we took all of their conveniences for granted. European elegance seemed artificial to us for it made a pretense of luxury but it did not have many of the physical comforts that we were used to. In the Far East this contrast was even more startling.

But this was only part of it. Our people learned to haggle over prices when buying souvenirs abroad in a manner they would not consider doing at home because somehow the rules and the ethics were different over there. There was a feeling that in a lot of places most public officials had their hand out and it was not uncommon to have to pay somebody to get service that should be routinely available to everyone. While bribes were not unheard of in the States it was something you knew some people resorted to in order to get what they were not entitled to, and not something you had to do to obtain routine services. Yes we earned our reputation of arrogance. We really felt that we were better than anybody else. We lived in a world where we always felt that goodness would prevail and we were the good guys. You could always tell the white hats from the black hats. Let others bend the rules we were secure in the knowledge that ultimately we would triumph. The good old U.S. of A. was the greatest country in the world. We knew it and dammit we told the world about it.

World War II came upon us suddenly. A sneak attack that was supposed to cripple us once and for all instead brought us together like never before. All wars are bad, there are no good ones. But if it wasn't obvious before, this war showed the world what we could do when we pulled together. And pull together we did. Yes ours was a lucky generation to have seen this country at its best. It still brings a lump to my throat to remember those days of grim determination, of joint total effort, and underneath it all of quiet confidence. It's an America our younger generation does not know. It's an America we sometimes forget. It's an America that except for that brief moment when Neil Armstrong took his "giant leap" we have not seen since. The words are the same. We agree that this is still the greatest country in the world, but we don't say it with the same conviction a before.

And we have pushed into the background the thoughts of the America we have learned to adjust to. The America of Watergate, the Vietnam War, trade deficits, inflation, payoffs, budget deficits, and a weakened dollar. Our popularity around the world has not improved. The difference is that now we don't command the respect we once did. At home it is the era of consumerism in which our citizens are sold on the idea that their individual judgment is not good enough and that they need the protection of an ever-stronger government. More and more the question is asked whether democracy is failing, and certainly there are enough failures to point to. Nobody stops to think that democracy's only failure is to permit our form of government to change from what it was, to gradually resemble a socialistic system that has failed around the world. And that our present weaknesses or failures can be traced directly to what is socialistic about our government and not to what is democratic about it. Because people around the world never understood, and lately we at home seem to be forgetting, what has been the source of our strength. Even at the height of our supremacy, criticisms were heard about our government's irresolute and seemingly haphazard way of doing anything. To some it was a wonder that such a weak government could get any results at all. They just didn't understand that our inherent strength came from the personal liberties that we enjoyed. That those were personal liberties that we did not relinquish to anybody and especially not to our own government. And the results were a strength and stability worthy of their envy.

But relinquish them we have, and thus our strength has waned. The process has been gradual and subtle, but unrelenting. American ingenuity, self-determination, individuality, self-reliance, independence have been systematically replaced by an increasing dependence on government to solve our problems. "There ought to be a law" is our answer to every problem.

We appear to have forgotten that the more we depend on government for all the essentials of life, the more we approach a totalitarian system of government. We have forgotten that this country was born and prospered because our people treasured and defended their individual liberties. We have forgotten that anything that you relinquish to the government, the government never gives back. We have forgotten that anywhere in the world that you find oppressed people, it is their own government that is the oppressor.

SOUL SEARCHING

Any process of analysis must have a well-defined objective or it becomes pointless. To isolate deficiencies or weaknesses here and there serves no purpose unless we can go the extra step of grouping our findings into logical categories or discernible trends that may help us in identifying the causes of the problem and in pointing the way to possible solutions. Two problems have become obvious to me as the principal areas of concern.

In the first place, economically we no longer hold the position of undisputed leadership we once enjoyed. It's not just that the other powers of the world have gotten better. Predictably that was to be expected. European industrial nations can mass-produce their good quality as efficiently as anybody, and Japanese quality today has made everybody forget their previous reputation. But the fact that others get better and stronger should be a plus and not a minus. The real concern is that while they went forward we seem to have gone backwards, and it is now our quality that is sometimes suspect and our prices that are not always competitive.

The second area we should examine is the breakdown in moral values. It is not just the increase in the incidence of crime. That appears to be a world-wide phenomenon. Of bigger concern is the breakdown in the basic family structure, a discernible change in attitude about moral obligations, a prevalence of corruption in business and government, a gradual erosion of the difference between right and wrong, and the growing lack of acceptance of responsibility for our own actions.

Added to this and perhaps the worst part of all, is the acceptance by all of us of these evolving changes in our way of life. It doesn't seem to bother us that as the government grows, our choices become less. More and more of the things that each individual used to decide for himself are now mandated by our ever stronger government.

Don't we care? Don't we stop to think that this is a one-way street? That the rights we surrender we will never again recover? You know, if we chop down a tree in the rain forest in Brazil, that single act probably has very little significance. But if we continue to chop trees indiscriminately, sooner or later we will do irreparable damage. And it will not do any good then to try to pin point at what time or which tree took us to the point of no return. Like the proverbial straw that broke the camel's back we may someday wonder which law caused us to say that we are no longer a free country. Let us look at the big picture here.

Every country in the world strives for economic prosperity. People have to be fed and housed. Means of transportation must be provided, and the struggle for survival must be eased so more and more people can enjoy a comfortable existence. The point is that the objective, the target, the goal, is always economic prosperity. The dreams of Utopia always begin with an abundance of all of the basic necessities. It is only after all of these have been provided that other comforts, entertainments and the arts can be enjoyed. And just how do you go about obtaining this economic prosperity?

There is no easy answer to that question. Economists around the world offer many different approaches in search for every possible solution. This exercise is not intended to provide an economic model that would insure prosperity. But we must examine the roots of the problem if we are to have a logical starting place. And so, I concluded that even though the search for economic well-being encompasses different theories and methods, there is one ingredient that I believe most people will agree is indispensable: WORK.

No country can achieve prosperity unless the majority of its people are productive. A country can be rich in natural resources and thus the task may be easier and well defined. Or it can be lacking in many of the basic ingredients and this makes it harder for its people. But in both cases, work they must. And a way has to be found to insure that the bulk of the population becomes productive and that the smallest possible portion of the population becomes a burden. So how do you do this? Just how do you make sure that most people will get down to work?

In only one of two ways: You force them to work, or you give them an incentive to work. It is that simple. There are no alternatives. And there is the inescapable truth. You find a system that will preserve the dignity of man or you turn him into a slave.

Written on the Statue of Liberty is the symbolic poem by Emma Lazarus which includes the famous lines: "Give me your tired, your poor, your huddled masses yearning to breathe free..."

What a great invitation! What it is really saying is give me the ones that are tired of tyranny, for they are the people who cherish freedom and are willing to work in pursuit of their aims. Or in other words, give me the one ingredient that I need, for those are the people that made this country great. The people who, having suffered under a strong government, saw in our constitution the protection that they needed to insure that the government would not interfere with their pursuit of happiness and therefore had all the incentive they needed to get to work. Take away that protection and the whole system breaks down. They didn't come for a handout. The incentive was the opportunity to work in an environment free from the threat of government interference. Let them begin to feel threatened by government and the incentive will be gone.

Nobody has come in one fell swoop, Pearl Harbor style, and taken away our incentive. Instead we are chipping away at it a very little bit at a time giving each time a small part of our liberties to the government in exchange for expediency. The process is so gradual that we have been adjusting to it without realizing what is going on. The result is an ever larger and stronger government with a corresponding loss of our individual freedoms. And it is the loss of those freedoms that if unchecked, will eventually and inevitably lead to the loss of our democratic way of life.

The other area is perhaps a little bit harder to pin down, but in my opinion has an effect that is just as devastating. It is truly appalling to see how far we have drifted from the set of moral standards that we grew up under and which we accepted as a matter of course as the normal pattern of behavior. And it all starts in the home.

I am one of eight children, and the importance of the family as the basic structure in our society is something I learned early in my life. Honesty is something that was drilled into us thoroughly by our parents and we were taught that it has nothing to do with the chances of getting caught, for if you have to be watched, then you are not honest. Later on, as I grew up Dad went on to point out that, in the business world, honesty was also good business. Once people know you they will come back time and again and feel comfortable doing business with you. What a wonderful world to live in this would be if most people understood and lived by these principles! But more and more we seem to be drifting farther and farther away from this Utopic world.

The business world is no longer a comfortable place. There is no place in business for a handshake agreement any more. The moral commitment is a thing of the past. A new set of moral values has gradually replaced the old one. Can it be that the principles of honesty and the difference between right and wrong are not being stressed early enough as before? Or is it natural to expect that they be more easily forgotten under the pressures of today's modern environment? Well, of course it's both. Nothing can replace those early teachings in the home. But many parents today just don't spend enough time with their children. In many households with both parents working or in single parent environments the task is admittedly harder, but the effort must be made or the results can be disastrous. The demands of present day life affect us in this and other ways.

When I left the army many years ago my first job was in insurance. During my early lessons in underwriting I remember being cautioned to watch out for "moral hazards". The classic example given to us at that time of a "moral hazard" was the bank teller who needs a small amount of money to complete his rent or mortgage payment, and yet daily he is handed thousands of dollars to work with all day long. It is so easy to borrow a small amount that he really intends to return in a few days. It's the kind of temptation that can too often start somebody down the wrong path. The classic example of a "moral hazard" that I would give today is the government official who finds himself to be the person who can grant or deny a permit, or who can delay or expedite an application, or who is in a position to overlook a minor violation or make a big thing out of it.

Our ever growing government bureaucracy with its myriad of regulations continuously creates in geometric progression thousands and thousands of similar situations where legitimate needs to expedite a procedure or to obtain a favorable interpretation turn into moral hazards. As more and more laws are put on the books and as more regulations become effective, the problem continues to escalate. From a minor inspector in the field to the halls of congress in Washington, temptation rears its ugly head at all levels. Again, the erosion has been oh so subtle, but devastating nonetheless. And the sad part about it is that it is a one-way street. Once the person takes that first wrong step he rationalizes himself into a gradually changing set of moral values. He kids himself into believing that a small tip to expedite something that he was entitled to in the first place is not wrong. Or that outsmarting the government isn't cheating. Or that cheating on his income tax is the smart thing to do, or that exaggerating his claim to an insurance company isn't dishonest. Or that taking the towels from the hotel is not stealing. After a while the end justifies almost any means.

And as our dependence on government increases, the importance of having a friend in the right government post increases the temptation to influence the election process. The words of Jean Jacques Rousseau come to mind: "--the abuse of laws by the government is a less evil than the corruption of the legislator..." Are we doomed to live in a world where the least scrupulous people in our community are the most influential?

I guess it is obvious by now that I have focused on the massive growth of government as the biggest source of concern. Why? Because government can only grow at the expense of our individual liberties. And if we are willing to give up our liberties then we are signaling the end of our democratic way of life. I firmly believe that the preservation of our individual liberties must be our main concern if we are to show the world that our democratic system can endure and be a model for people everywhere that would cherish freedom.

I certainly am not the first to worry about centralized power. There have been many voices out there warning the American people of the evils of an ever larger and more powerful government. The scary thing about it is that the growth process appears to be unstoppable. What I am trying to focus on are the reasons why it continues to grow disproportionally in strength and size. And recognizing that this growth inevitably continues to erode our precious liberties, the objective is to find a manner in which this process could be stopped or reversed.

I'm not concerned about the logical growth that comes from increased activity. It stands to reason that if the population grows, we may need more census takers. But the unrelenting increase in influence over every aspect of our daily lives must be stopped or "Big Brother" is the inevitable result.

I mentioned before that we needed specifics. We are not looking for fine-tuning here. There are many small improvements that can be made here and there. I probably won't resist the temptation of making some specific suggestions during the course of this exercise on other changes that may be more or less important. But what we really need is a basic or fundamental strengthening of our system that will keep us from going astray in spite of ourselves. We need to identify that one change that will prevent the balance of power from shifting away from the people to an ever-growing omnipotent government.

But lets start at the beginning. Why does this happen? What are the causes? Why have we allowed it? Who is responsible?

It would be a cop-out to say that we are all responsible although that is undoubtedly the truth. Human beings fortunately or unfortunately are human and as such are subject to human frailties. Human nature being what it is, we all have a very convenient memory. The lessons of the past no matter how painfully learned are quickly erased by the needs of today or worse still by the convenience of the moment. Every one of us who ever asked for a law to solve one of our problems has contributed to this process. But there is no way in the world that we are going to change human nature. We are always going to ask for relief at the slightest provocation. So we need to strengthen the basic structure of our system to preserve the principles of democracy in spite of our own recurring weaknesses.

The words in our constitution outline clearly what the role of government should be. "We the people of the United States, in order to form a more perfect union, establish justice, insure domestic tranquility, provide for the common defense, promote the general welfare, and secure the blessings of liberty to ourselves and our posterity..." Just how do we insure that government stays within those general boundaries? It is an almost impossible task especially when all of us continuously expand them by asking the government to regulate more and more things every day. No question about it we are all responsible, but for the purposes of this exercise I have selected several areas that in my opinion bear looking into for a better understanding of what is taking place.

BUSINESS

Since I have been a businessman all my life perhaps business is the first culprit I should examine. I remember in Puerto Rico back in the early 1970s, that a law was enacted creating a price control agency known by the acronym DACO[1]. It was given the power to set the price for all goods and services in the island. Its powers were so awesome that in some cases it was known to have permitted different prices for the same article at separate establishments, so that the director of that agency, if he so chose, could select which establishment would earn more money and which would have to struggle to survive. And from a practical point of view appeal was not possible.

The initial reaction against this law was widespread and resulted in the creation of an organization called *The Association Pro Free Enterprise.* It started to campaign very actively and at least initially apparently effectively for repeal of the law. Gradually however their enthusiasm waned. It seems that as the strongest supporters of the

---

1 *Departamento de asuntos al consumidor*

association obtained favorable rulings for the price of their wares, their militancy subsided. And one by one opposition to the law was effectively neutralized. A classic example of how our narrow-minded, short-term objectives cloud our understanding, and cause us to sacrifice principle for the sake of expediency. The political party that had sponsored that legislation was defeated at the next elections, but those who thought the law would be automatically repealed were disappointed. The only thing that changed was the name of the head of the agency.

You see, once you relinquish something to the government, it never gives it back. The law stands on the books to this day and businessmen have learned to live with it and in many cases like it, because, as long as the agency accepts their figures, it is the equivalent of operating on a cost-plus basis, and that is easier than having to compete. It is an example of what Walter Wriston in his book called government of men instead of laws. The power is there anytime the government wants to wield it, and we blithely tolerate it and even thrive on it because, for the moment, we are showing a profit. And we do not have to do a better job than our competitor to make that profit. The day that DACO decides to lower the boom on one particular individual or establishment, the rest of us will probably sit idly by and let it happen. It is a sword that hangs over everybody's head and it is there because we sacrificed principle for convenience.

Unfortunately this is not an isolated incident. Business has found ways not only to adjust to new regulations, but continuously sponsors and puts laws on the books throughout this land protecting their turf in every conceivable aspect of our daily lives. From banking to transportation to manufacturing to farm subsidies to trade protectionism, we operate an army of lobbyists in Washington that insures not only the continuation but the expansion of the process. And of course the government thrives on it. Every new law creates new regulations, which in turn require more people to see that they are carried out. The Government has never learned, or perhaps doesn't care that regulations don't keep people from breaking the law. And regulations in turn become an expansion of the law that inevitably punishes the innocent rather than the guilty. For it is the people that want to obey the laws that struggle with the regulations. Take the S.E.C. as an example of this. Everything in business that you say to the public must first be cleared by the S.E.C. before it is sent out or distributed. Presumption of innocence, you see, is something government regulators do not abide by. The idea that if you mislead the public, you must accept the consequences has never been enough for them. The attitude seems to be that all business people will defraud the public if permitted to do so (presumption of guilt) and so the innocent are penalized. In any publication there is no way to point out an advantage that your company may have without adding disclaimers to negate its value. And the "boiler plate" language that must be included is so vast that after a while, it becomes meaningless. It is very difficult to tell the difference between a good and bad company from reading a prospectus on a new offering because all of the language that must be included by both makes them read about the same.

Some time ago I was involved in the sale of the company I had been associated with. It was a fairly simple straightforward transaction that had been encouraged by many of our stockholders. The proxy material for our stockholders meeting turned out to be such a costly, complicated and voluminous document, that I was reluctant to send it out for fear that it would confuse rather than clarify things for our stockholders. But our S.E.C. attorney was quick to point out that it was not intended to be understood by the stockholders, but to placate S.E.C. requirements. I gave in and sent it to my stockholders and I have felt ashamed of myself ever since for having done it. Because it is the acceptance by all of us of this new bureaucratic way of doing business that is the larger problem.

In 1978 under President Carter the first steps were taken to deregulate the airline industry. I was surprised to hear that the most violent opposition came from the airline industry itself. I should have known better. They were very comfortable in their protected environment. If they could get monopoly routes or exclude others from invading their market area, that alone would do more to assure their success and profitability than improved service or creative marketing strategies. But the problem was bigger than that. You see, it's not just that they found it easier to lobby than to compete. The sad part is that their organizations had gradually been structured to do just that, and they no longer were prepared to or ABLE to compete. Other people in the world still remember how it is done. I had occasion to visit the Far East some years ago and everybody gave me the same advice: If you get the chance to fly Singapore Airlines do so, they have the best service. I followed the advice and sure enough the service was excellent. I don't remember if the fares were more expensive or not, but I remember deciding that I would prefer to fly them again anytime I had a choice.

How could we have drifted so far away from what used to be our trademark? What a role reversal for American business! Is this the land of free enterprise?

What about my own industry of banking? We are typical of what is happening throughout business in America. Our top management more and more is made up of lawyers more concerned with regulations than with customers, more concerned with compliance than with service.

When I first moved to Miami, I was involved on behalf of our bank in the negotiations to acquire a small bank in Miami. It was a friendly and cordial transaction and on the day of the takeover, I was asked by one of the members of the selling group, if I would like to be a part of an industry advisory committee that he belonged to. I was pleased and flattered by the invitation because the people we were dealing with were very highly regarded by bank regulators and in fact by the community in general. As a newcomer to this market, I quickly envisioned this as a good first step. I found myself rapidly backpedaling however, when he explained that state regulators were underpaid and that, but for their committee, they would not be able to travel in style and bring their wives to conventions and other activities. It was a shocking introduction to the realities of what can happen when the permits you get from the government become more important than the service you provide to your customers. And sadly enough, too much of this type of thing can be found throughout all of the business community.

And again I tell you, that it is our acceptance of it by all of us that is even worse than the situation itself. For if we lose the willingness to compete, if we lose our individuality, if we lose that spirit of independence that we once cherished, then we've lost the essential ingredient for success in an environment of freedom and dignity.

TELEVISION

The impact that television has had on our thinking and on our entire way of life cannot be overemphasized. I will not try to dwell on all of the ways in which this powerful media has affected us, but I will concentrate on only two of the effects that it has had which I believe are pertinent to our analysis and objective.

More than any other single thing television is responsible for the deterioration in the structure of the American family. Let me explain. Before the days of television, a small child's primary source of information was his parents. Never mind whether the information was always correct or not, consider the relationship. As a child, when I needed to know something, I went to my dad or to my mother. I expected them to know everything and, more importantly, I naturally accepted every answer. Subconsciously I looked up to them. It strengthened the ties between us and my feelings were of high admiration and respect. I still remember that in later years when my dad said something that I believed might be in error I went back and rechecked my facts, and if I still thought he was wrong more often than not I would not contradict him out of respect. But that was before television. Since the advent of television, and long before the internet, the normal reliance on the parents has suffered a drastic change. Practically all of the information comes from the box and too often every time the parent opens his mouth he gets an argument. A child is quick to tell his father that he is wrong and quote something heard on television to lend strength to his argument. It is an erosion of the very foundation of the home.

The breakdown in moral values in today's society can be traced in large measure to this weakening of the family structure. Every child comes into this world with no knowledge, but with a fertile brain avid to absorb the teachings available to him. Not everybody reacts the same way, but by and large a child will learn what he is taught. The formative years are critical and will determine in large measure his worth to the community for the rest of his life. I know from my own experience that most of my deep-rooted ideas can be traced to those early teachings.

To illustrate; until the eighth grade I attended a public elementary school that fortunately was located only about a block and a half away from our home and on the same side of the street. The first time that I was allowed to walk to school by myself I was instructed that every time I needed help outside the home, I was to seek out a policeman. It was drilled into me that every policeman was a friend and could be counted on for help. That image of the police as a friend was deeply ingrained and has stayed with me to this day. It is only recently that I have pondered what my feelings might be today if policemen had been portrayed as an enemy?

Parental guidance is essential. Any erosion of that relationship can have devastating effects. Somebody coined the phrase "quality time." It is a cop-out for people who do not devote enough time to their children and would like you to believe that somehow they get the same result in short bursts. My friends, this is one time that quality is not as good as quantity. It is the day-in and day-out dedication that is needed and there is no substitute for it.

And just what are our children exposed to when they peer into this spectacular TV window that gives them a glimpse of the world. In the first place, television is an indiscriminate dispenser of a new morality. Talk shows bring into your living room discussions on such subjects as teen-age sex, living together over marriage, contraceptives, abortion, unwed mothers, gay rights, prostitution, and many others. In the scramble for viewers' attention, rebellious youths are glamorized, challenging of parental authority is often encouraged, and more responsible youngsters are ridiculed as "nerds." And violence is everywhere. All in all, it depicts an environment of irresponsibility that creates a formidable challenge for dedicated parents.

More subtle perhaps but just as real is the gradual erosion of the difference between right and wrong. No matter what the subject, you can always find somebody with an opposing view. Controversy means ratings and every controversial subject is debated endlessly for all to hear. Every violent or illegal act turns up with somebody to defend it. And everything we thought was good, finds somebody to tear it down. In an attempt to at least give the illusion of fairness, both sides of every issue are debated even if the producers of the program had to scramble to find somebody to support a minority opinion. As a result, television too often rather than teaching and clarifying is adding to the confusion that abounds in the minds of our growing children.

But the youngsters are not the only ones that can be confused. The other aspect that I would call to your attention is the tremendous influence it can have on the political process. Television clearly is more powerful than any other medium when you're trying to sell a product or more importantly an individual. What a tool for a political campaign! And it does not always act as responsibly as you would like. The "hype" that probably started with professional wrestling matches and later extended to other sports, has continued its expansion into other subjects. It is a matter of routine now to air so called documentaries designed specifically for "image building." Forget any aspirations of being elected to public office if you do not have a well-orchestrated television campaign. The famous Nixon/

Kennedy debate many years ago made it obvious to all, and the costs of running a successful campaign have been soaring ever since. Too often, the man elected is the one with the biggest budget.

No question about it, television more than any other single thing has changed our entire way of life and unfortunately not always for the better. But I don't know that anything can be done about it. Somebody suggested to me that political commercials should not be permitted. That it should be alright to permit debating of the issues and to permit other television time on legitimate newsworthy endeavors, but not the type of image building commercial that has become the vogue in recent campaigns. But that clearly is not the answer. We are looking for ways of strengthening our democratic system and any restrictions of any kind of an individual's right to compete is not the way to go. Television may have good or bad effects, but if we are going to have a free society, we must let public acceptance of programming be the only criteria for determining what goes on the air.

And now we have the Internet.

INTERNET

We are living in very interesting times. New technological discoveries are announced all the time and old folks like me can't really keep up with the rapid pace and the many changes that affect our everyday living. I guess in times gone by breakthroughs such as electric lights must have been just as momentous, but the rapid pace and the sheer number of new discoveries, makes me think this is an era like no other.

My son learned to fly at the age of sixteen, and even though as parents we worried every time he left for the airport, it was rewarding to see the happiness flying would bring him. It was very evident in a short poem he wrote at that time.

Alien World

The air is calm...
Then all at once the hellish thunder
Dooms that peace, as the man-made wonder

Reaching up for the cherished skies
Struggles free of its earthbound ties.

The seconds pass…
And with each second the awesome beast
Subdues its roar and feels at ease.
Once again the silence reigns
In this strange world of ethereal plains.

The man looks out…
And sees the ground where eagles play.
He pierces mountains in his way
knowing the bird in which he dreams
Will bow to satisfy his whims.

The sun goes down…
And, all too soon the sojourn ends
Ending thus the peace of men.
Screaming curses, graceful turns,
Alerts the world of its return.

The night is black…
And both the man and faithful friend
Wish they were up aloft again.
For once the man has learned to fly,
This alien world will not suffice.

I must conclude that the younger generation, probably has that alien feeling about the way of life we were used to, but I must admit to my own alien feeling in trying to adjust to this strange new world.

Much as television affected every household and the relationship between parents and their children, the Internet has now widened the gap. Don't get me wrong, I recognize it as progress. The incredible accessibility of information, the opening of so many new forms of communication, the opportunity to expand interrelations with people all over the world, and the promise of new things to come make me realize the wonder and the excitement of the moment. But I worry that in the speed of this new environment the new generation may not realize the importance of basic tried and true principles. A solid foundation for every project is something that was drilled into me early at home by my parents and confirmed time and again at different stages of my education.

The only sport I was ever really good at was fencing. At West Point I was fortunate enough to have Jack Diamond as fencing coach. Even on my last year when I was captain of the team and we were in the middle of competition, he would give me a lesson at least four times a week. He would take me back every time to the fundamentals correcting me on my stance, position of the head, my hands, my feet, in fact slowing me down to review every move.

It's a lesson I'll never forget. Everything we do, no matter the method employed, must have a solid foundation. A rock-solid set of principles and ethics based on high moral values.

My great grandchildren and all of their friends know computers and the Internet better than I do. It makes me wonder if kids today not only believe they know more than we do, but also believe that there is no reason for them to listen to what old folks like me have to say. If somehow our insistence that no matter the methods employed, tried and true principles are still valid is falling on deaf ears. Will they take to heart the concept that everything they do must have a solid base of ethics and morality?

The Internet of course is, in a sense, making the world smaller. We are in communication with people from all over the world like never before. I've got to believe that is a good thing. And yet it makes me wonder if cyberspace traveling may be having the effect on the younger generations of gradually losing some of that strong feeling of " love of country" that a lot of us have felt so strongly all of our lives. I am fortunate to have done some traveling during my lifetime and to have visited many places in at least four continents. Some places I have liked better than others, but in every place there was always something to admire and merit my respect. But my country is my country. A feeling nothing could take away. And yet I fear that their travel may have a different feel. Every one of my trips inevitably reached a point at which I just wanted to get home. No matter how good the trip, happiness was back at home. The fact that they are doing it from the comfort of their own home deprives them of the feeling of homesickness. You miss and appreciate things the most when you don't have them.

One thing that scares me about the Internet is that it is both intrusive and anonymous. Maybe it is just ignorance on my part, but I get the feeling that many of the things I do are being monitored. But whether that is true or not, there is no doubt that more and more our privacy is less and less. And yet what scares me the most is to think that a lot of our young people may be regularly talking to and maybe even following instructions from somebody they may have befriended on the net. Somebody who, not only they have not met, but who might be misrepresenting himself.

I mentioned before the role that television now plays during the costly election campaigns that are such an important part of our democratic system. Another scary thought is how the Internet may be misused in the election of our public officials. It not only gives more opportunities for foul play in the actual casting of votes, but also may be used to hide where campaign contributions are coming from. In every campaign candidates inevitably become indebted to persons or organizations that have become strong supporters. That is not new. But the idea that we may have no way of knowing the source of that support is of concern. I read in the newspaper that during the last presidential campaign the candidate that later was the winner received contributions in the amount of about one hundred and fifty million dollars during the course of just one month. It made me speculate that powerful interests might be the source of much of that amount, and they might later be expecting somehow to collect on the strength of their contributions.

I recognize and applaud the progress that the Internet represents. Progress is progress and adaptation to changes has been an on-going process throughout the world since the beginning of mankind. But here in the U.S. as we adapt to each new environment, our task is clear. The methods we employ will continue to change as we take advantage of evolving technology, but our objectives don't change. We must insure that the foundations of our system of government are strong and sound and able to preserve for us the individual liberties we cherish.

CONSUMERISM

I guess one of the hardest things to control is the natural instincts or impulsive outbursts of John Q. Public. We certainly cannot blame an individual that is faced with a problem for seeking relief anywhere that he can find it. "There ought to be a law" is too often the only answer that he can think of. The old saying "The road to hell is paved with good intentions" I believe has a direct application here because well meaning individuals and organizations inevitably spring up to take the initiative and spearhead the drive to enact laws for every conceivable protection they perceive the consumers may need.

Undoubtedly there are inequities out there, but there are many options available to individuals without transferring their rights to an ever stronger government that proceeds to give so called protection to all whether they want it or not. How some people feel qualified to determine what's good for somebody else and subject us all to that kind of universal justice has always been a source of wonder to me. Yet that seems to be a compulsion that too many of us find hard to resist.

I recalled Quero's patient explanation of the elaborate plans for a managed economy. It was of course based on the theory that only the people at the top were qualified to determine what was good for everybody. The idea of self-determination by each individual about his own priorities was unacceptable. Unfortunately in this country more and more we are allowing that type of thinking to replace free market principle.

One of the many examples of this, which I deplore, is in professional sports. In an attempt to achieve balance among teams, there is something called the draft. The best athlete in a particular sport is forced to go to the worst team in the league. Where is the freedom of choice here? What about that athlete's constitutional right to negotiate with the team of his choice? And what about each team owner's right to compete freely for the best talent? The idea that they will achieve better balance and thus better competition among teams by restricting the ability to compete for the best athletes goes against every principle that is cherished by our people. If a franchise does not do well in open competition then it should fall by the wayside and be replaced by a more aggressive force in the marketplace.

Sports may not seem to be the most important area of concern, but it serves to illustrate how prevalent this type of thinking is becoming in our country. Too often all of us appear to fall into the delusion that we should make the decisions for somebody else about what is good for them. For me, this lesson came early.

When my oldest daughter graduated from high school, she took a job as a computer programmer. She promptly came to see me with a business proposition. If I would buy her a car, she would take care of the insurance and expenses. The alternative was to have her borrow my car so I thought that I had made a good deal when I accepted until I was faced with a similar request from my son who was in college at the time. Having bought his car, my sense of justice took over and I offered to buy one for my other daughter who was just old enough to get her license. You know, I never did buy that third one for the simple reason that SHE DID NOT WANT ONE. She had her own priorities. I believed myself to be generous and fair but I was forced to learn my lesson that no matter how well intentioned or how generously inspired, there were a lot of choices that I had no business trying to make for her.

It's the mistake totalitarian governments make all the time. Even if they had the best intentions and the most noble purposes, how can anybody sit in judgment at the top and determine what is good for everybody or for that matter, for anybody? This is the beauty of our democratic system. Individual choice, and the emphasis is on the word individual. Milton and Rose Friedman summarized the essence of democracy in the title of their book *Free to Choose*. It is that individual freedom that makes us different. To surrender any part of that freedom is to start on the path to surrender.

That's what I have against the Ralph Naders of this world. The fact that consumerism, in practice, ultimately serves only to increase the price to the consumer, makes the whole thing a futile effort. But, the real damage is the gradual erosion of each individual's right to determine what is good for him.

That right to make his own individual choice is precious. The right of an individual to make his own mistakes. I may disagree with somebody's choice, but I've got to respect his right to make it. I may have been surprised by my daughter's decision but, after I thought about it, I realized I should have given her the opportunity to let me know what she liked or needed rather than assuming that she would like the same things as the others. Individual choice is precious. It is the essence of freedom. It is the backbone of our system of government. It is what pursuit of happiness as spelled out in the Constitution is all about. Respect the right of others and each individual can feel free to act in his own self-interest.

But mandated consumer protection continues its inexorable pace to include almost every aspect of our daily lives. Some things are more important than others, but the principle is still the same. For instance, I agree with the requirement to protect children properly when traveling in an automobile. Until they are mature enough to make responsible decisions for themselves, it is our obligation to see to their safety. But why am I forced to fasten my seat belt? I probably would do it anyway because I have been informed that it is safer to do so and it seems to me to be a logical procedure. But as long as it is something that affects only me, it should be my choice and not an obligation by law. And now I understand I will be required to purchase health insurance whether I want to or not, or whether I can afford to or not. That one is worse. After all I could avoid the seatbelt requirement by just not riding in a car, but there is no way to avoid the new one.

Universal justice? Are we all being drafted to march to the beat of the same drummer? What is happening to individual choice?

ATTORNEYS

The legal profession has to come in for its share of the blame. No other group as a whole (other than government itself) has benefitted more from the escalation in government influence. Logically, the ever growing myriad of regulations and the ever mounting red tape requires a group of specialists to keep track of and sort out for us, all of the new wrinkles in the law that we are expected to comply with. We have more attorneys today than ever before and still we have trouble understanding and complying with the law.

Law firms are more numerous and larger than ever and attorneys abound in the ranks of upper management in the corporate world. Unfortunately, in its rapid growth, the legal profession has lost its perspective or perhaps a little of its sense of direction. As a result, it is contributing to the deterioration we have been deploring here. You see, we expect lawyers to help us determine what's legal and what's not, We depend on them more than we depend on doctors to keep us healthy. We call a doctor when we get sick, but we call the lawyer before we buy, or before we sell, or before we negotiate, or before we do anything. And increasingly they get us into trouble instead of keeping us out. They contribute to our confusion as to what's right and what's wrong because in their own training and in the pursuit of the technicalities of the law, they have forsaken the concept that some things are right and some things are wrong and that it is important to be able to tell the difference.

I read a book some time ago titled "Best Evidence." It is one man's probe into the assassination of President Kennedy and he takes the reader through his analysis of the evidence in an effort to reach conclusions other than those found by the Warren report. There is a point in the book where he believes he has irrefutable evidence which contradicts the official findings, and he places this evidence before a group of law students hoping to get them to back his theories. He is flabbergasted to find that they are inclined to throw out some of his most devastating facts. He proceeds to analyze the thought process followed by the group and reaches the conclusion that lawyers just think differently than the rest of us for the simple reason that they have been taught that way.

To a lawyer, the only truth is what a court of law determines the truth to be. They are taught to argue both sides of a question equally vehemently and accept the finding as the truth even if others may think that particular decision absurd. In this book the "best evidence" was determined to be the autopsy results and all evidence which contradicted those findings was arbitrarily thrown out. If this analysis has any merit at all, then it's no wonder that the difference between right and wrong is becoming a thing of the past.

If we can argue on both sides of every legal or moral issue, if we can justify either course of action, if we can consult with counsel and feel we can defend any decision we make, then it is understandable that we are developing a new set of values. It is easy to see why moral commitments are becoming a thing of the past. It is all part of this new morality. We depend on attorneys to make the laws, to lobby on our behalf for more favorable laws, to interpret the laws for us, to tell us how to get around the laws, to plug up the loopholes attorneys find in the laws, to find new loopholes on the strengthened laws, and to champion our cause when somebody's attorney has a different interpretation than ours. It is not surprising that more and more we are seeing the top management of the big corporations being saturated with people with a legal education.

I guess we still have to compete for business up to a point, but if we can get a protected route or a protected franchise from Washington, it makes the task easier and so we put the emphasis on the lobbying and the regulations and on the task of getting along with the regulators all to the detriment of the consumer who suffers from the corresponding decrease in service.

Affecting the whole picture are the changes that have taken place over the years on the judicial system especially as it refers to all civil litigation. A number of years ago, the rule makers determined that it was only fair to have both parties in a lawsuit know ahead of time what evidence the adverse party will present at trial time so there will be no surprises and he can prepare properly. Business has never been the same since. It is no longer possible to get justice in the courts today. Every litigation becomes an interminable series of so called discovery proceedings that are used regularly to delay and harass the other party. Any lawsuit of any importance will take literally years of litigation with legal fees very often escalating beyond the original controversy. It borders on a form of legalized blackmail. The fact that you believe yourself to be in the right or that your case is a strong one has to take a backseat to the realities of time and efforts to be expended as well as to the costs involved. Lawyers bemoan the situation but blithely continue to profit from it. And if we were worried about moral hazards before, consider that they are the only ones who profit and they are the ones we go to for counseling.

I had a situation one time when somebody started to buy stock in our company on the open market in quantities beyond any normal investment. He filed a 13D report with the SEC as required but giving away nothing as to his intentions. I consulted with counsel to see if we could get more specific information. His answer was that there was a way that we could get all the information that we wanted. By filing a lawsuit against him a different set of rules would apply and we would then be entitled to discovery proceedings. Needless to say that's one advice I did not follow. The man had done nothing but buy our stock which was something I always interpreted as an act of confidence in our company, and it just did not seem right to me to react in that manner. But you see, I don't believe the attorney interpreted that pointing out what was right and what was wrong was any part of his job, but only to tell me how we could get the information we wanted.

I have no suggestions to offer for attorneys. Again I feel they have to be free to pursue their own self-interests. I will, however, make some comments on the judicial system that I feel can be improved considerably. They are part of those fine-tuning suggestions which are not our primary objective in this book, but which I anticipated I could not refrain from making.

I have no better solution than trial by jury for criminal cases. Imperfect as it is, I don't know of anything that is any better. I do have one suggestion to make. I would eliminate all peremptory challenges. If there is no valid cause for eliminating somebody from the jury, then he should not be excused. The practice of fencing around trying to get a favorable group is nothing but an attempt to influence the results on other than the evidence presented.

This brings me to another moral hazard I have encountered. When I moved to Florida, I was surprised to find that judges were elected and not appointed. My first time at the polls, I was confronted with the task of selecting which candidates to vote for from among a list of names most of whom were totally unfamiliar to me. The next time I tried to be better prepared, but although I then was able to recognize the names, I still had no idea who really was better qualified for the position. Judges have to campaign like other candidates and, of course, need campaign contributions. This means they have to go hat in hand soliciting money from people that someday may have to appear before them. And, of course, the biggest contributions can be expected to come from those more likely to find themselves in need of a friendly judge. It would seem to make more sense to have a blue ribbon panel study the records and qualifications of the candidates and make the appropriate recommendations to the appointing authority preserving in this manner the integrity of the system and the objectivity of the new judges.

POLITICIANS

Nobody is in a better position to affect our way of life, for better or worse, than the people we have elected to public office. Presumably most of our elected officials started their entry into public life with noble purposes and visions of accomplishments worthy of recognition by all. Unfortunately, in too many cases that does not last very long. To start with, the campaign for election is the first obstacle. The competition to win that position requires, not only financial, but also influential support. And this evolves into making promises and making deals that later may become obligations if elected. Obligations that not always are in harmony with the lofty goals he or she may have started with. Words are a politician's forte, and promises are his most potent weapon. Promises that once elected they may not be able to keep, or too often are merely conveniently forgotten. The result is that politicians in general have a well-earned reputation for being even less truthful than used car salesmen.

Once in office even more deal making is in store. He needs support for what he wants to do, and others need his vote for their own agenda. Deal making is the only way to get anything done so it becomes routine to settle for the "political" solutions. Problems still have to be dealt with and there is a lot of work to be done. It dawns on him that there is not that much time to accomplish many of the things he wanted to do. So the emphasis changes to extending his term of office. In other words, reelection becomes the first priority. And this is true at all levels. In addition, for elected officials the position becomes addictive. Whether they admit it or not, career politicians subconsciously enjoy their position of power and they know it is the best job they will ever have.

At the time of this writing, our current president has been in office a little over one year, which means that there are still more than two years to go before his active reelection campaign. But I read in the newspapers earlier this year how he had to attend a fund raising event in New York and more recently he came down here to my state of Florida for a similar purpose. I have no idea how much money was raised for his party at either place, but I know that every time the president travels it is a very costly proposition for the tax payers. I've mentioned how expensive running a political campaign can be. But there's no question a sitting president has a distinct advantage. No wonder that incumbents have such a good track record at election time.

PRESENT ECONOMIC CRISIS

Up to this point I have been expressing my concerns about the inexorable growth of our government and the gradual erosion of our individual liberties. Lets now take a look at conditions today and see what effect these negative trends are having.

Our country has been going through a very difficult economic situation for the past few years. A great many people have lost their homes and their jobs. And this comes at a time when one of the biggest campaign promises made by our newly elected president was the creation of four and a half million new jobs. Our president has told us time and again that this is a problem he inherited. For once I agree with that statement. The U.S.A. is a very big country and its economic trends don't turn on a dime. When things are going well the incumbents are quick to take credit, and when problems are in evidence inevitably the finger pointing begins. The truth is that every new president is inevitably faced with a myriad of problems and, though it is important to ascertain origin and cause, the emphasis should always be on appropriate course of action and making sure he is making things better and not just pointing out that they are inherited and not his fault.

In this case I agree with our president when he says the problem already existed by the time he took office. I just don't think he pointed his finger back far enough. Our real problems go beyond the recent housing and unemployment problems.

When I was in school, our President was F.D.R., and it seemed to me that he had been there forever. His "New Deal" was the starting point on the road to eventually becoming the welfare state we are evolving into. The erosion since then has been very gradual, but unrelenting.

This country became the greatest nation in the world because its citizens cherished their freedom. Freedom from what? From unwarranted government intervention. Our citizens consist in large measure of immigrants who came here to get away from an oppressive government. They did not come here for a handout. They came for the opportunity to work "in pursuit of happiness", as promised by our Constitution. They understood the role of government as protection of its citizens. They saw that protection as the only real function of the government. They knew their individual liberties were the rock solid foundation of our system of government, the roots that made everything grow. They took great pride in saying that this is a free country.

But we can no longer say that. Call it paternalism. Call it welfare. Call it socialism. It is no longer the land of opportunity. And our ever-growing government is going broke. All of the so-called entitlement programs are so costly that they are unsustainable. And what has our president done with his inherited problems? He is adding new ones. Despite many warnings and much opposition, he is forcing new legislation that again takes away some of our individual choices and aggravates the problem. And how does he propose to pay for it? That he has made clear. He will take it from the rich.

President Obama has done something that to my knowledge no other president has ever done. Regardless of party affiliation or the problems of the moment, all his predecessors have worked assiduously to maintain unity in our nation. But he has deliberately divided the country casting himself as the champion of "Main Street" against the "Fat Cats" (his words) of "Wall Street". Our own president fueling the fires of class wars within our country? It's hard to believe. How does he expect to create millions of new jobs when he is openly declaring war on the job providers?

Main Street and Wall Street are the same, or at least inseparable partners. When they work together, everybody benefits. Why would anybody want to drive them apart? The idea that the unemployment problem can be resolved by government stimulus to small business while continuing to put additional regulatory burdens on larger corporations may serve some political purpose, but will do very little to solve the main problem.

It is not just the number of people large corporations employ directly. They give life to a great number of small entrepreneurs. We also have to consider suppliers and subcontractors, as well as the myriads of small businesses that spring up around them – cleaning people, security, laundries, beauty parlors, pizzerias, restaurants, barber shops, stores of all kinds – the list is endless.

It is hard to fathom that somebody as intelligent as President Obama would not have a clear understanding of this. It leads me to the scary thought that he may have a completely different agenda. Our president seems to want the government to be all things to all people, and has a plan to pay for it. The kind of plan that professors in a classroom might draw up, the kind of professors who deal only in theory knowing they will never have to make their plans work in practice.

I wonder what I would do if I were the head of a large manufacturing plant considering expansion plans. Would my love for this country lead me to submit to all these difficulties and build here, or would common sense and the obligations to my stockholders lead me to build in one of the many places around the world that are trying to lure me over there with promises of concessions and a comfortable, business-friendly environment?

My Dad taught me passionately to love this country and, though he passed away many years ago, not a day goes by that I don't miss his sage counseling. And yet for the first time I am glad he is not here now to see what is happening.

Our president apparently believes that it is only fair to take it from the rich to pay for the excesses of this ever-growing government. Forget about pursuit of happiness or enjoying the fruits of your labor. Redistribution of wealth. Where have I heard that before? I'd hate to think Quero was right. But all the misgivings I have felt throughout the years appear to be having a snowball effect and seem to be crashing down on us. Maybe we should take a little time here to examine the causes leading to our present economic problems.

CHICKEN LITTLE

I always try not to jump to conclusions when I am not in possession of all the facts. But too often all the pertinent information is not available and I can't help but speculate and even draw my own conclusions especially in matters of importance.

In the year 2008 it became obvious that our country was facing serious economic problems and there was wide speculation about the causes and about what, if anything, should be our course of action. I expected the government to explain with some detail the facts of the problem we were facing, but we were told only their conclusions and we were forced to make our own speculations about the seriousness of the situation. Listening to Treasury Secretary Paulson and President Bush on television, I could not help but think of the story of chicken little.

I am not sure if it is true, but I always thought the story came from one of Aesop's fables. In any event, it is a tale of a chicken that has an acorn fall on his head and jumps to the conclusion that the sky is falling, and is joined by all the animals in his trek to give the king the bad news. A picture formed in my mind that Mr. Paulson believed the sky was falling and somehow convinced the president to warn the nation.

As an old commercial banker, I know we don't just need a sound banking system, we need the confidence of the general public. We need for everybody to trust the banks and feel safe in dealing with them. It was a scary moment to hear our President on television telling us that the economic problems facing the country were so bad that the entire financial structure was in danger. I could understand their concern, but even if the situation was as bad as they feared, I knew that scaring the nation in that manner was not the thing to do.

I am not suggesting that bad news should be withheld from the public. On the contrary, I believe more details should be made available about the nature of the problem and not just the scary conclusion that the nation was on the brink of disaster. More details that would allow us to see for ourselves if the sky was really falling or if it was just an acorn. I guess maybe they felt that the thing to do was to over- dramatize the situation in order to push congress into acceding to their requests. I presume the congressmen were given more details. In any event, they responded and approved the enormous amount of about seven hundred billion dollars to buy troubled assets from the financial community.

I am not sure if this money was actually used exactly as originally intended. A new administration took office at the beginning of the year 2009 and the decision was made to use these funds to bail out a number of troubled companies. In my opinion, this action was unwarranted. Of course there was cause for concern, and of course, there were measures to be taken by the federal government. But if we believe in the free market system, we must trust it to function and deal with its problems.

I agree with some of the measures taken by the FED such as feeding liquidity into the market, lowering rates, and broadening the activities of the FED discount window. And I agree that there are other things they should do. But the notion that the government had to bail out private companies is ludicrous. That is a case of the cure being worse than the disease. The free in free market means freedom from government intrusion. To violate that, means our financial markets are no longer free. And free is the essence of our system of government.

I have been stressing the need to somehow curb the continuous growth of our government, but the serious economic problems that developed turned out to be the driving force (or maybe the excuse) to accelerate the expansion and intrusion of the federal establishment. New expressions crept into our everyday speech, like "systemic risk" and "too big to fail", and the money appropriated by Congress found its way to bail out a number of institutions including banks, investment houses, insurance companies, and automobile manufacturers.

I am not sure that "bail out" is the appropriate term. Maybe in some of the cases, the troubled institutions might have gone into bankruptcy, but clearly not in all of them. In one case the money was said to have been forced on the recipient, and in another the offer of assistance was actually turned down by the company concerned with the assurance that it was not needed. And of course in each case conditions and controls were imposed over and above the payment of interest and the issuance of stock options as a kicker.

In order to get out from under some of those new controls, a number of banks proceeded to make arrangements for early repayment of their loan. For some obscure reason, the federal authorities apparently were not anxious to have the money repaid, so they devised what they called "stress tests" to determine if the banks concerned were financially strong enough to make the repayment. The test results were that some could and some could not. This repayment was seized upon by the government officials to claim success in saving the taxpayers money telling us how much profit had been obtained in those particular loans. It gave me some measure of confirmation that those so-called bailouts should not have been made in the first place.

As of this writing, a new financial regulations bill is being debated in Congress and the rhetoric states that it is intended to prevent future breakdowns in the economy such as the one we are still trying to put behind us. I heard on the news that the bill being considered is over thirteen-hundred pages long. If that is true, it scares me to even think what they really expect this new law if approved to accomplish.

I said before that it is wrong to sit in judgment without having all the facts. But this is one time that I don't need all the details to know this is a mistake. I am sure that some of the people voting on it don't even know everything that is included in there. And you do not have to be a genius to know that thirteen-hundred pages of additional regulations will do more harm than good. For sure, it will make the federal government bigger and stronger, and, of course, it will reduce further our individual liberties.

The present economic situation is clearly the worst we have experienced in the last ninety years. Maybe we should examine more closely how we got here before we decide on the measures to be taken. But perhaps we should start by examining the S&L crisis we suffered through some years ago to see if we can detect any similarities.

S&Ls

Congress created the federally chartered savings and loan institutions as a vehicle to provide home mortgages on reasonable terms for prospective home buyers. They were all started as mutual associations which meant that [in theory at least] the legal owners were the depositors themselves. The standard savings account contract was what we called a "share" account, meaning that the depositor owned a share in the institution and was entitled to one vote at the annual meeting to select its board of directors. It also meant that if and when the association was dissolved, he would be entitled to a share of the surplus funds of the institution. These savings accounts would earn interest as approved by each institution's board, but interest rates were regulated by the Government so that savings and loans could pay a rate that was at least one half of one percent higher than the rates permitted to be paid by commercial banks. In this manner, the savings and loans could be assured of funding at a reasonable cost for the mortgage loans they were expected to make.

For a number of years, the system worked admirably well. In my opinion there were two reasons for this early success: In the first place, the nature of the share account contract. In a commercial bank, a savings account has a provision that gives the bank the option to require thirty days notice for withdrawal of funds. This option in the normal course of business was never exercised, but its existence differentiated it from funds deposited on demand and justified the payment of interest for monies in savings accounts. Share accounts went further. Recognizing that money deposited would be invested in long term mortgages, the share account contract gave the institution the option to require somebody asking to withdraw his funds, to wait until the association liquidated its investments no matter how long this might take. Normally again, this option was not used, but its existence permitted the institutions to forget about liquidity problems and proceed to make loans, usually for more than one hundred percent of their deposits.

The other reason was the simplicity of the whole operation. They had savings (share) accounts and they made home mortgages. Very little else. No high priced talent was needed and the clerical help in these institutions became very proficient in these routine transactions. I remember an officer from our bank that left us to go to work for a large savings and loans institution. About two months later, he invited me to lunch and told me he was bored to death. He had a large office, a secretary, and nothing to do.

Maybe it was because I was a commercial banker, but even at the height of their success I disliked the structure of the savings and loans institutions. The idea that the association belonged to its depositors was in my opinion a myth. The usual practice was to take a perpetual proxy from the depositor at the time the account was opened thus perpetuating the board of directors. And when an account was closed, no credit was given for any share of the surplus funds of the institutions, which meant that those funds were owned by only those depositors who happened to be there at the time the institution were dissolved. The typical board of directors usually included the attorney that closed the mortgages, an insurance man, a property appraiser, somebody who provided credit reports, and maybe an advertising person. I was used to having the directors in our bank clearly representing the interests of our stockholders and it always seemed to me that the savings and loan board members described above had to have different motivations.

Unfortunately, as effective as the system was, the savings and loan industry was not satisfied with what they had. They wanted faster growth and they wanted to expand the scope of their activities. When certificates of deposit started becoming popular, the S & L's saw their opportunity. This was something they could do that would allow them to compete aggressively and grow faster and they jumped right in. Of course, CD's are not share accounts and the depositor has the right to demand his funds at maturity and the institution would have no option but to honor that request. But still, little if any consideration was given to improving liquidity. It was a fact that apparently was also overlooked by the regulators. Borrowing short to lend long with no provision for adequate liquidity is a sure invitation to disaster. When interest rates went through the roof, a lot of S&Ls found themselves in serious difficulties. The rate they had to pay to renew the certificates as they became due, exceeded the rate that they were receiving from their mortgages. It was an industry-wide problem and the regulators were reluctant to take the drastic measures it called for.

After some time, a creative solution in the case of mergers or acquisitions, and later in all cases, was found. You could restate your mortgage portfolio to reflect true market value which would create a sizable loss, but instead of showing a loss, a "good will" asset was simultaneously created by the same amount. Instant solvency. The losses were deferred over a number of years and the institutions ended up with increased capital. I remember an article in the Miami Herald extolling the virtues of the restructured Centrust S&L (across the street from our Miami bank), which then showed a tangible net worth of one hundred and twenty million dollars and was poised for expansion. The figures also showed a newly created "good will" amount of five hundred million dollars, which, as far as I was concerned, meant three hundred and eighty millions in the red.

But this creative solution did not solve the problem. They were still operating at a loss, and to correct this a new solution was needed. Commercial banks seemed to be doing much better, so the solution then was to expand the powers of the S&Ls to make them resemble banks. This they did, and soon many S&Ls were plunging into different businesses that they were ill equipped to deal with. The result was that the better managed institutions fared better, but a great many of them went much deeper into the hole.

The biggest mistake in this whole fiasco was not the granting of additional powers to the industry, but rather, aggravating the magnitude of the problem by the attitude of the regulators. For one thing, they failed to realize the need to provide for more liquidity when funding for their mortgage portfolio was expanded to include reliance on certificates of deposits. C.Ds they should have recognized, are a form of borrowing that must be limited to the capacity of the institution to repay. And then they failed to act decisively at the first sign of trouble. Bad as it was, at the initial stage it was something they probably could have handled.

With the deposits insured up to one hundred thousand dollars, a new type of business developed for money brokers. They would offer their services to large investors and corporations to invest their money in CDs (insured by the US Government) and distribute them one hundred thousand dollars in each of the highest paying S&Ls throughout the country. And of course the highest paying ones were inevitably those with the biggest problems. Eventually the marketplace weeded out the weaker ones and normalcy was restored. But it also signified the end of S&Ls as a separate industry as the surviving institutions gradually became more like commercial banks.

I think there are two lessons to be learned from this whole experience. In the first place, **basic principles can't be ignored**. Every time you make a change in the way you conduct your business, it is imperative to study all the possible consequences. Especially so if the change involves borrowings or in any way overleveraging of your position.

And in second place, we must learn that government regulation does not prevent these things from happening. The regulator can monitor the operation, express their concern about different matters, and impose restrictions in the case of unsafe practices. Also, of course, they can ensure compliance with the law. But it must let the company conduct its business without undue interference. The government cannot be a back seat driver.

TOO BIG TO FAIL

In the early nineteen-eighties, I was heading a small commercial bank in Miami, Florida when the news came out about one of the two largest banks in Chicago being in serious financial trouble. It was the first time I heard the expression "Too big to fail", which was the determination made by the government.

The F.D.I.C. quickly let everybody know that the government was prepared to support the bank, and that it was safe to continue to do business with that bank. Not everybody responded to that announcement as well as they expected, but we jumped at the opportunity.

A normal part of our operations included what was called "sale of FED funds", which meant that every day any excess cash over what was required to be on deposit with the FED would be loaned overnight to another bank. We promptly increased the amount that we would lend to Continental Illinois to the maximum allowed, and enjoyed having that practically risk-free facility. And, it didn't hurt that the F.D.I.C. was happy with us for responding to their request to help them out.

However, even though we profited from the situation, it never ceased to bother me. I am a firm believer in the free market system. It is a self-regulating system. It rewards the good operators and punishes the weak ones. It is important to remember that the **loss side** is just as important as the **profit side**. The idea that the government will bail you out if you fail, destroys the basic principles that make the system work. It rescues the poor operators and inevitably forces the good ones to pay for the cost of the bailout. Let me explain.

Every businessman is faced with the same type of decisions every day. Each situation or opportunity requires a three-part analysis. First, what is to be gained? If it's attractive, then the risk involved must be considered. Of course, we know that higher profit usually means higher risk. So the other two parts of the analysis must be determined. Is it a reasonable risk, and can you afford it if things don't turn out as you expect?

Too big to fail is an invitation to irresponsibility. It tells you that you only have to worry about the first part of the analysis. How attractive is it? If it is, it's telling you to "go for it" knowing that you have a safety net if you stumble.

I am not suggesting that this was the sole reason that caused the big economic troubles that our country has been experiencing, although I believe it certainly was one of the many contributing factors. My concern is that it led us down the wrong path in trying to correct the problem. We say that we believe in the free market, but we did not trust it enough to allow it to work. I understand the desire, in the face of a dire situation, to step in and do something. But, this is a case where the cure is worse than the disease. Of course, the market solutions would have been painful, but probably not more so than what we have endured this past year. And certainly the long-term effects would have been more satisfying and longer-lasting.

In difficult times the government always has an important role to play. The many things it can do merit a new analysis completely dedicated to that subject. For now it is important to remember that bailing out failing private institutions is not one of them.

WHAT HAPPENED?

The present crisis was triggered by two separate events. The first one, of course, being the collapse in the real estate market, especially residential homes. We all should have seen that one coming. Why? Because it has happened more than once before.

When demand exceeds supply, prices rise and suppliers rush to replenish inventories. This is true with all articles. But in real estate, the time lag in construction of houses creates a larger problem. It just takes longer to realize that the demand now has been exceeded. At that point there are units in different stages of construction that have to be finished to preserve their value. This process inevitably takes many months during which costs of construction and carrying interest continue to rise even after proceeds from sales has virtually stopped. Inevitably the emphasis then shifts to trying to sell the excessive inventory to repay the large financing which was needed for the construction.

As I said, this has happened before, only this time it was more excessive and dramatic. I recall just a few years ago my son telling me of a conversation with one of his friends who is a real estate broker. He told him the story of a house he had sold three times in less than three years at higher prices every time. In that period of time the price had more than doubled. We commented at the time that this seemed to be the general trend in this part of the country.

When you stop to think about it, the bursting of that bubble was inevitable. You know that the income of the prospective buyers had not doubled in the same period of time and had to have gone up only a small fraction of that if at all. That means that a couple looking to buy a one hundred and fifty thousand dollars house now was faced with a three hundred thousand dollars price tag. The buyers needed the homes and had to commit for more than they had budgeted for, and to help them, the sellers came up with creative ideas like adjustable rate mortgages.

Meanwhile the lenders had rushed to get in on the real estate boom. They not only loaded up on mortgages, but in search for more leverage they bundled together groups of them and sold participations of these groups to other lenders or investors.

When the supply started to exceed the demand, two things became apparent. Sales almost stopped, and mortgage delinquency started rising. And this was so throughout the entire country.

This brings us to the second cause. Homeowners everywhere were overextended and were having trouble paying not only for their mortgage, but also for all other bills. The first result of this was that they started maxing out their credit cards. Massive credit card delinquencies on top of the mortgages problem really aggravated the situation and increased the strain on the whole financial system.

Credit cards; what a trap. This is something that I mentally struggled with for many years during my banking career. Back about 1970 commercial banks all over the country were going into the credit card business. Before then credit cards were mostly T&E (travel and entertaining) cards and the leaders were American Express and Diners Club. At that time I was with the largest bank in Puerto Rico, which had earned its reputation in that market as the leader in new systems and innovations.

We had a very good officer in the bank who saw the trend in the U.S., did his research, and urged us to get a credit card program going ahead of the other banks. But I was reluctant and delayed the project. He left the bank soon after that and joined our closest competitor where he proceeded to launch a successful program of Visa cards. He later on would leave that bank and become a senior executive of Visa International.

There were two things about the system I did not like. In the first place it meant an open-ended loan authorization to almost every bank customer. In addition, I did not like having to set up what I saw as a parallel system in our computer center to start billing our customers for their purchases. My son was head of research and development at our bank at the time and he came up with a solution to both of my objections. "There is no need to bill separately," he said. "When the charge comes in from the merchant we can just charge our customer's account." What an idea! We proceeded to do so and the result was that back in 1973 we had in operation what I believe was the first debit card system in all of the United States.

Credit cards are a trap for the consumer. Talk about a moral hazard. Its very convenience lures the user to overextend himself. And the inevitable interest and other charges become the equivalent of a sales tax which makes every purchase more expensive.

There were probably many other contributing factors to the economic woes which have plagued the country, but these two are what I call the triggers. And they both have a common evil that is the main problem: OVER-BORROWING.

As you can see it was also a factor in the S&L crisis previously described. No doubt about it, excessive borrowing is risky. It is risky for individuals, for institutions, and oh yes for the government. As it rushes to expand its controls in its race to be all things to all people, the costs of this ever-growing government are reaching unsustainable levels.

Our government's own economists are warning that the social security program is not properly funded. We already knew that the costs of Medicare and Medicaid could not be continued much longer. But instead of working on proper solutions to those problems and disregarding many warnings, we rushed into what could be called nationalization of all healthcare that inevitably will increase the burden on the national budget. And now comes this new thirteen hundred page financial regulations bill which inevitably if approved, will require additional expansion of our already massive bureaucracy.

Our regulatory systems I believe do need looking into. But the first step should be to arrive at a clear understanding of what we are trying to accomplish. The notion that we can prevent future economic problems by piling on more regulations is at best, naive. Regulations do not dictate the course of events. So what really should we do?

In the first place we should take a look at what we have in place now. I read that one of the objectives is to limit the size of certain institutions to prevent the problem of "too big to fail". In my opinion a free market would take care of this problem one way or another without any government interference. In any event, don't we already have monopoly statutes? I've also heard that we need a resolutions entity to handle large failures. What about our present bankruptcy laws? We certainly do not want to duplicate what we already have.

I was never too fond of monopoly laws. I recognize that if an institution gets big enough in the sales of their product to gain a large market share, it could feel tempted to engage in unfair market practices to squeeze out the smaller competitors. But, I believe what is bad is to allow those unsavory actions. Bigness alone should not be considered to be bad. After all, the institution probably achieved that large customer base by providing good prices and good service. The idea that big companies should be broken up or down sized just because they are big goes against the very essence of the free market system.

The government should concentrate in watching for all wrongdoings. Pursue vigorously all the ones that act improperly, but be a friend to the ethical successful entrepreneurs.

While we are on the subject of monopoly laws, I could never understand why Big Labor is not subject to the same laws as business. If the three largest automobile manufacturers get together to establish prices, they are clearly in violation of the law. But, unions can have the same person calling the shots for the whole domestic industry without being subject to the same restrictions.

When I was with the bank in Puerto Rico, one of our customers was *Caribair*, the only certified airline on the island, and as airlines go it was one of the smallest airlines in the U.S. And yet, they had a lot of trouble in trying to negotiate labor contracts. Why? Because, small as it was, it had five different unions to deal with. The pilots, mechanics, stewardesses, baggage handlers, and office staff all belonged to different unions at least three of which were national unions that negotiated the contracts for practically all the airlines in the mainland. Every time a contract had to be renewed, a representative of one of those unions would come down from the mainland, probably the same person that negotiated with airlines like United or TWA. This person could not think of making any concessions that might later be used as a precedent when he would have to negotiate with the big airlines. The specific needs of that particular small company had to take a back seat to their big picture. The employees of Caribair could certainly have used the services of a union that would represent exclusively their interests. That certainly was not the only problem they had, but the fact is the airline went bankrupt and eventually was taken over by Eastern Airlines.

As an old commercial banker, the regulator that I am most familiar with is the F.D.I.C. I always try to examine fundamentals, and this is one case that I feel is based on sound principles and has a history of good performance. It has been the practice by the media lately to lump together all financial institutions as one and the same. In reality, there are some functions that distinguish commercial banks from all the others. Specifically there is the payments system which is carried on only by the banks in partnership with the FED. As a result the population in general is practically forced to depend on the services of the banks. The trust of the people in the commercial banking system is essential.

The banking system must be sound, and the insurance provided by the F.D.I.C. plays an important part in helping to add peace of mind to all bank customers.

If it insures the deposits, then it is logical that they must monitor and examine the banks they are insuring. But wait a minute. Did you know that they do not get to examine all the banks they insure? A great number of banks are examined by the Comptroller Of The Currency and I believe others by the FED.

One of the important purposes of having regulators is accountability. Who is responsible for early detection of problems? Of course the F.D.I.C. receives copies of the reports prepared by examiners presumed to be equally as competent as their own. But, having to depend on somebody else's work lends itself to blame avoidance in case of problems.

By the way, I'm not sure what exactly the Comptroller of the Currency's duties are. I know that he charters and monitors national banks, but why? I really think that when the FED came into being, they assumed all of the comptrollers functions and there was no longer need for federally chartered banks. All of our paper currency now consists of Federal Reserve notes, instead of the gold or silver certificates, which were previously issued by national banks. I know that the government does not like to give up anything they have, but unless there is a necessary function that I don't know about, that is one department I would abolish. It certainly would be easy enough for national banks to change to a state charter.

Accountability should be the focus of regulations and in my opinion, for this purpose, less is better. The practice of piling up additional layers of supervision just has the effect of diluting responsibility. And when you put two different functions together you run the risk of creating conflicts of interest as in the case of the FED. Their main function is monetary policy and in difficult times like these, they may want to urge the banks to lend more. But when you add supervisory duties they may need in that role to urge banks to be more cautious. There is no way that he can sacrifice one duty for the other one. I would relieve the FED of all regulatory duties and have them concentrate on their primary function of monetary policy.

It was never my intention to try to spell out what financial regulatory reform should look like. I mentioned before that I probably would not resist the temptation to make suggestions here and there to address specific problems in areas I am familiar with. In truth, there are many things that must be done. Fortunately, in this great country we have a wealth of talent and a great many people that would like nothing better than the opportunity to contribute in some way to the solving of our problems.

My purpose was always to focus on the necessity to get ourselves back on track. We should accept the fact that the welfare state does not work and will inevitably lead us to financial ruin. We must learn not only from our own mistakes, but also from what we have seen elsewhere. At this time in Europe all the countries are rushing to save Greece from financial ruin, but already other larger countries appear to be on the same path.

We have seen how individuals have over borrowed and lost their homes. We have seen how small businesses have failed under heavy debt. And we have seen how over leverage has put some of the largest corporations in jeopardy. And now we see countries in Europe having their troubles for the same reasons. Do we think we are immune?

I think it is time to take action. What should we do? How can we start? How can we proceed to reclaim our individual liberties? Who can do that?

WHAT SHOULD WE DO?

Up to this point I have been expressing my concerns and trying to sort out and identify our most flagrant needs. And I have spent most of my time studying how all of us must share the blame in contributing to allow our government to grow at our expense. In the process of assessing the problems we face today, I have purposely refrained from even mentioning the fact that we are at war. We have many of our young men and women overseas, in harms way, fighting to protect all of us and preserve our way of life. There are two reasons for avoiding that important subject. In the first place the war effort deserves our undivided support. Comments and opinions should be deferred until we hopefully have a satisfactory conclusion of that conflict and our troops return home. The second reason is that, while they are out there fighting for us, we at home have to do our part on their behalf. The purpose of this exercise is precisely to attempt to match their effort. They are fighting to preserve our freedom and it is up to us to see that we don't lose it at home. To insure that their sacrifice has not been in vain.

Of course, the war effort is expensive, but that is not only necessary, but it is a logical use of our financial resources. Why? Because that is the primary function of government: protection of its citizens. Some people might say it is the only function if we are to call ours a free country.

I am not trying to minimize the serious economic problems we are facing at the present time. They have to be dealt with. But I am endeavoring to focus on the big picture and on finding a feasible plan of action to bring us back to the course we have been straying away from for the last eighty years. And that means to begin the task of correcting our course, to steer away from the welfare state.

We have to return to the principles that this country was founded on. To reclaim our individual liberties. To redefine the limitations that *"We the People"* must put on our government.

I stated earlier that the words of Quero seemed inconsequential. Maybe I was wrong. He told me clearly that they were infiltrating our education centers, our communications media, and our labor movement. In the course of putting my thoughts on paper, it struck me that it was too much of a coincidence that the outlook of so many of our citizens now seems to be to depend on a strong government for everything. It makes me wonder if this socialist doctrine is part of what our kids are being exposed to at our universities.

People are no longer willing to accept responsibility for their actions. People are not willing make the extra effort because they expect the government to provide for them. In so doing, they have forgotten the feeling of satisfaction and pride obtained from accomplishing something through their own efforts.

So many people now think this way, that we have elected a president who, in his first year in office, proceeded to divide our people. A president who openly follows the Marxist ideology of redistribution of wealth. What a scary thought!

Our situation today cries for immediate action. But, stop-gap measures seem to me like the little Dutch boy trying to stop the leak in the dike with his finger. The magnitude of the problem calls for well thought-out solutions.

Too many things have to be done. It will require the well-coordinated efforts and expertise of well-meaning citizens from all walks of life. Fortunately, in this great country there is a vast amount of talented people who would jump at the chance to do their part. How can we give them the opportunity to do just that?

WRONG ROAD

The incredible new technological advances of recent years have given us more information about every conceivable subject than we ever had before. That should be a good thing. Unfortunately, one of the consequences of this information overload, is that we now also have more opinions about everything than ever before. We are continuously bombarded by a myriad of conflicting suggestions on how to solve every problem, big or small.

Attention to detail is important in performing almost any task. But, looking in all directions at the same time, makes it impossible to recognize the correct path to follow. I'm reminded of the old cliché about being so busy studying the leaves that we can't see the tree. We have to look at the big picture, and we must have a clear understanding of what our ultimate goal is. The crew of a big commercial jet airplane preparing for takeoff have a lot of tasks to attend to. But, none of these mean much unless a final destination has been established.

Should we tax more? How about another stimulus package? Maybe we should reduce expenses. What about the minimum wage? What should we do about "Obama-care"? The list is endless. And meaningless, unless we first define clearly what our objective is.

Somewhere along our journey, we lost our way. We took the wrong road and are now traveling at great speed, but in the wrong direction. We seem content with listening to suggestions on how to avoid the potholes we're encountering in our way, without realizing that all the suggestions in the world can't help us if we're headed the wrong way.

Our country's expenses are out of control, and things are getting worse. The costs of our entitlement programs are already unsustainable, and growing more and more every day. Our national debt keeps increasing. Interest rates, which are currently very low, will inevitably increase, and when they do, the interest burden on our debt will increase alarmingly. Unemployment continues to be high, with no solution in sight. In short, our current situation is serious, it is affecting everybody, and we cannot afford to waste any more time.

In order to have a permanent solution to these problems, it is essential that we get back on the right road. But, the urgency of our economic situation requires that we follow a two-step plan.

First, we have to get our economy functioning on all cylinders again. The second step does not have to wait for the first one to be completed. From day one, we must start to reverse the downward spiral we find ourselves in.

Let's deal with that first step first. How do we create more jobs? Who can provide them? Clearly, not the government. Jobs… permanent jobs… good jobs… can only come from the same place they always have – the private sector. But, business does not seem to be doing much hiring. In fact, we have seen more outsourcing or plant expansions outside the country than we used to. Why?

There are many places around the world that are luring U.S. businessmen and companies. And the formula is simple: no taxes, low-cost utilities, maybe free land to build on, and most importantly, the assurance of a business-friendly environment. But, wait a minute… that invitation has been out there for a long time with no takers. Why is it different now?

It used to be that the heads of large American companies simply felt more comfortable doing business in the good old USA, the best country in the world. But, these same businessmen have now become scared. It's not so much that the climate abroad has improved, rather the domestic business environment has become less attractive. Businessmen see the government getting involved in just about every aspect of their businesses and they are rightfully concerned. Everybody is waiting for the next shoe to drop. What else will be coming out of Washington? What new regulations are they going to have to contend with?

Our President has gone out of his way to say that small businesses are desirable, but large corporations are the enemy. He has convinced the general public that Wall Street is responsible for our economic woes… that rich is bad. In his campaign against large companies, he even wants to limit what successful companies may pay their executives, or even investors.

The rewards derived from success used to be the incentive that motivated everybody, and fueled the economy. Why this campaign to remove that incentive? Why is it so difficult for the President to see that it is precisely Washington's negative attitude towards business that is responsible for the so-called "exporting of jobs"?

Our task is clear. We have to re-unify the country. Wall Street and Main Street are not enemies… they are partners. They need each other. They feed off each other. The direct payroll of a big company is important, but it is only part of its worth to the prosperity of the community. The company needs suppliers, sub-contractors, and service people. As a result, hundreds of small companies spring up around them: restaurants, laundries, flower shops, dry cleaners, beauty parlors, etc.

When Wall Street and Main Street work together, everybody benefits. When you drive them apart, as the President has done, everybody suffers.

It seems to me that it would be relatively easy for the President to correct this. He started it, and he can reverse it, although I don't think he will. Why? because, by his actions, he has shown that he doesn't believe in the free market system... the very same system that played such a big part in making our country great.

I hope I'm wrong, because our job would be easier if he were on board. But, I'm afraid it's going to be up to us to insist that our congressmen do whatever is necessary to change the current anti-business attitude of our government.

This is the first step, and it is essential. The only way to improve our economy is for business to prosper. Not just small business, but ALL business. And that can only happen if we restore a friendly business environment in our country.

The second step is more fundamental, and therefore more challenging. We need to get back on the right road. We need to once again set our sights on our destination. We need to re-discover who we are, and make sure we start moving in that direction. The path we are on is not the path that led us to become the greatest nation in the world. Where did we go wrong? Where did we make a wrong turn?

We became great because we always kept government in its proper place. We became great because our Constitution protected our unalienable rights by establishing "we the People" as the supreme law of the land. To this day, whenever the Supreme Court is asked to rule on whether or not specific actions of the government are constitutional, they often rely on the "original intent" of the framers to make their determination.

Maybe that's what we should do now... to look at everything that's happening and determine whether the government's current actions are consistent with the intent of the framers when they drafted that powerful document. Did they envision the country becoming a welfare state, where the government seeks to be all things to all people? Or, did they intend for the Constitution to our protection against a government's ability to take away our choices and our rights?

Like it or not, those are the only two options... individual freedom, or government control... self-reliance, or depending on the government... making our own choices, or asking the government to make them for us.

We have our work cut out for us, and it's not going to be easy. Too big a part of our population expects the government to provide for them, and it's going to be a monumental task to change that way of thinking. To change from a "Welfare State", to the "Land of Opportunity" we used to be. And, it's going to take time, because it has to be done right.

The USA cannot default on existing commitments to its citizens. But it is imperative that we stop making additional commitments for the future.

I'm afraid this undertaking requires more than just communicating with our congressmen. We cannot allow politics to keep us from getting the job done, because we're going to need the help of all concerned citizens. I certainly don't have all the answers, but, as I mentioned before, there is a lot of talent in this great land of ours. We just have to find a way of giving everybody who wants to help the opportunity to do so.

A PERMANENT SOLUTION

In his classic work "The Politics" written more than 300 years B.C., Aristotle starts out early in the book establishing some basic principles in this manner:

"We shall, I think, in this as in other subjects, get the best view of the matter if we look at the natural growth of things from the beginning. The first point is that those which are ineffective without each other must be united in a pair. For example, the union of male and female is essential for reproduction, since each is powerless without the other; and this is not a matter of choice, but is due to the desire, implanted by nature in both animals and plants, to propagate one's kind.

Equally essential is the combination of ruler and ruled, the purpose of their coming together being their common safety. For he that can by his intelligence foresee things needed is by nature ruler and master, while he whose bodily strength enables him to perform them is by nature a slave, one of those who are ruled.

> *Thus there is a common interest uniting master and slave."*

This relationship between ruler and ruled which he likened to master and slave is an inescapable fact that has been haunting mankind throughout history. The struggle to be the master and not the slave or the ruler rather than the ruled has been the source of violence throughout the ages. Experiments in democracy have not always been completely successful for the simple reason that in everyday living, the ruler and the ruled still exist and the relationship though moderated remains basically the same.

It is for this reason that the U.S experience started out to be something so special. The idea of elections every so often to see who would rule for a limited period of time was not new. But to make the highest law of the land a constitution which would draw its power directly from the people and LIMIT THE POWERS OF THE RULER turned out to be the key ingredient that gave birth to the greatest nation the world had ever known. And it is this same constitution that still holds the key to preserving our way of life. Because "We The People" have to go back to that Constitution and redefine what the roles of the rulers in this government of the people and by the people should be. Our own apathy has permitted, these rulers to evolve gradually into the classic role of masters. And the process must be reversed before our own roles evolve into the classic roles of the ruled, which is slavery.

When I resigned from the Army back in 1949, my commanding general told me when I said goodbye that he hated to see me go but that he understood my reasons for leaving. His one word of advice was that no matter how successful I became, I should take time out sometime for service in government. It seemed to me strange advice at the time but I believe that I now understand what he meant. He understood that IF THIS IS TRULY A GOVERNMENT OF THE PEOPLE, WE THE GOVERNED BETTER TAKE AN INTEREST IN OUR GOVERNMENT TO MAKE SURE WE HAVE PUBLIC SERVANTS DOING THE WORK RATHER THAN RULERS. And that means we who understand that difference must be willing to take our turn as public servants to preserve the integrity of the system.

But, aren't there enough people who are eager to serve in government? Why should we give up our valuable time when there is no shortage of people willing to dedicate all of their time to public service? I'll answer that with another question. Are these the people we want up there? If it is a sacrifice for some of us to dedicate some of our time to this end, who are these people who would give all of their time to government service sacrificing all civilian activities or endeavors? Let's see if we can understand their motivation.

These are people who have chosen "public service" as a career, forsaking all other pursuits in civilian life. They are what I call "would-be rulers" rather than public servants, and, in my opinion, no longer qualify as adequate representatives of "We the people." Their primary motivation is reelection, continuation in power. This goal comes before all others. It is the reason that good solutions sometimes don't have a chance because they are not good "political" solutions. It is a ruling class that has crept into the system and now controls it. It is a class I would abolish.

F.D.R. was elected to four consecutive terms for president. Despite his popularity and the successful outcome of the war, the dangers of perpetuity were recognized and "We the people" took the necessary steps to make sure this never happened again. I believe a similar remedy must now be taken.

An amendment to our constitution that would permit a person to run for office, at any level, not more than once in his or her lifetime, would effectively accomplish this. This would insure that every elected official would be a bona fide representative of the people. Such a person would necessarily have attained some measure of success in some civilian endeavor, whether it be business, labor, education, a profession, entertainment, communications, or any other. And his effectiveness during that one term in office could not be lessened in any way by time spent trying to perpetuate his temporary position of power. He would know that he must eventually return to his civilian endeavors, a fact that would hopefully encourage him to do the best job possible during his brief turn at bat.

It has been suggested to me that limiting people to only one term of service is a little drastic, that it doesn't allow for continuity, and that serving one term at the local level should not preclude that person from holding a position in the federal government.

However, I believe that limiting public service to a single term is essential to getting us back on the right road. That one term of service should be a sacrifice that an otherwise busy person would be willing to make on behalf of his/her country. It is the only way to insure that we truly have public servants in office, and not would-be rulers.

Passing a constitutional amendment to do this is not easy. Nothing worthwhile is. But, if enough people recognize this as a good permanent solution to get our country back on course, then it can be achieved.

There have been several attempts in the past to implement term limits in different forms, but all these attempts failed, at least in part, because we were depending on the very people who would be most hurt by their passage, namely legislators.

However, our modern means of communications, especially in the form of social media, provide us with a new opportunity to take up the cause of term limits once again. We now have the power to begin a grassroots movement in the true sense of the word; to inform the minds of "We the people", to unite our efforts, to share our hopes for a better future, and to communicate our concerns and aspirations to those who are supposed to be looking after our interests.

Social media has been much maligned and criticized, but it can also be the means for setting our democracy in action once again by placing the proper limits on those who serve our great country... a worthwhile endeavor indeed.